SONGS OF CHAOS

SONGS OF CHAOS

BILL SUTER

NewPlainsPress.com

Copyright © 2020 by Bill Suter

All rights reserved. No part of this book may be reproduced in any manner whatsoever without written permission except in the case of brief quotations embodied in critical articles and reviews.

First Printing, 2020

ISBN: 978-1-7345719-5-0

Bill Suter 1959–

Published by Agreement
Summerfield Publishing
New Plains Press
Auburn, AL
newplainspress.com

The prose poem "Letter to Another Country," as it appears in its current form, was published in Volney Road Review in September 2020, and we appreciate the review allowing it to be published in this volume.

Any resemblance to actual persons, living or dead, or actual events is purely co-incidental.

CONTENTS

A Marriage Of Heaven & Hell	1
Angel	2
Mister & Missing	3
Under The Lighthouse	4
Pretty Poison	9
On The Downside	11
The Way Goes On	13
The Apostle's Erection	14
Stepford Lives	15
Underground	16
Sign Language	17
The Mad Story Of A True Man	18
Marionette	20
Witness	21
At The Gate	22
Gulliver	23
Eye Of The Zombie	24

Rearview	25
Into The Air	26
Cinnamon	27
Fallen	28
Twilight	29
Bird Of Perfect White Silence	30
American Dream Therapy	32
Letter To Another Country	33
When Beauty Met The Beast	38
The Conversation	40
Sleep Studies	43
War Games	44
Imaginary Lover	45
Auto Focus	46
Outward Bound	47
The Beloved Object	48
City On The Edge Of Forever	49
Tragic Kingdom	51
Island Of Lost Luggage	52
Sympathy For The Devil	54
I Am The Night. That Is My Name.	56
Baghdad Cafe	57
Epitaph	59
Absurdistan	61

When Parallel Lines Intersect	63
So Far Away From Here	64
Dialogue	65
Statesman	67
Creditorial	69
Buried Pleasure	70
Triptych	71
The Stone Garden	73
Fable	74
About The Author	76

A Marriage of Heaven & Hell

Writing in a style that befits you
like costuming the flesh,
forms a carapace of elegance
draped in dreams afresh.

In this quiet conveyance,
a hundred wonders play,
pressing themselves together
in the most alluring way.

There is no hope of resistance,
you're drawn to the dance again,
soothing the sacred hunger
with the rhythm of paper and pen.

Angel

I've got this ache
deep in my bones, and
I need your help
to chase it away–
it was this inspiration
that led me here, and
you are the night
of the following day.

Caress me, my angel,
so beautiful,
the earth can neither
alter nor contain–
this sinuous lady
and her sweet delights, and
you are the night
of the following day.

Time has entangled
the ghostly dawn
that was born to wander,
and begs to stay
deep in the cavern
of a perfect night–

And *you are* the night
of the following day.

Mister & Missing

Are you, perhaps
the jealous sort,
fiercely protective
of your misery,
thoroughly enamored
of your martyrdom,
a sea of red droplets,
a fantasy?

Last I remember
the souls of men
bore burdens,
wept heavily and grieved,
and neither the heavens
nor the host of hell
condescended and
made you
the masochist's deity.

Hope you find
the country of young men, and
learn to caress
the tender flesh,
plucking from the
faulty optic nerve,
stigmata that have stolen
what we call *blessed*.

Under the Lighthouse

Thank you for coming with me. I don't think this story wants to tell itself, really, I...

Then you tell it. Was this where he fell?

No. Yes. Really, he jumped ... Donnie ... he made his great escape from here.

And this is the first time you've been here since then?

Yeah, a year ago. A year and a day today.

So you came here to...

To see if I could get to the other side of this...to find an answer, peace, healing ... no ... I don't know. The last time I saw a ribbon slide through the wind it tangled in a branch. I thought that's how he'd look, torn to pieces on the rocks, draped over stone. But he wasn't there.

Well ... where was he then?

I'm not sure. Vanished, "slick as a well-turned phrase." That's something he used to say. He could be magic with words, as if they were an itch in his brain he needed to share. Full of words, full of ideas, fearless, but ... easily swayed. Impressionable.

Gullible?

No, no. The opposite, really. If he believed something, it became a religion for him. I think it occupied time and space. Like God. His gift was convincing us his dreams were real ... and sometimes ... his nightmares.

I'll never forget his great revelation that virgin blood could make him levitate.

You mean–drinking blood?

Yeah. They sent him to see a psychologist after he bit this girl on the neck. He said over and over as they led him away, "I need to drink girl's blood! I need to taste blood!" He left school for a long time, but eventually–

He came back?

As if it were all a dream. He would say he was wrestling to express his vampire avatar: his nightmare, Lugosi, Dracula self. He was convinced, obsessed, and very unapologetic.

And you think this is how people overwhelmed with stress shed their skin? Fantasy?

Maybe. I'm not sure. I don't believe the obsession ever left him. From nine years old on it possessed him.

And then?

And then we came here because he said he heard a legend that things–anything–tossed from the top of the tower were misplaced, lost, transformed? I don't know, but we came here and lobbed a few quarters over the rail of the lighthouse. We couldn't see exactly where they went ... they drifted off course and we lost them, even in the glint of an overcast sky, they ... vanished.

So, what did Donnie do afterwards?

He fixed his eyes over the railing, hesitated a second, told me how close the ground seemed; then he smiled. "Watch this," he said, "I'm magic."
And he jumped. And I ... froze.

And that's when he vanished? Like the coins?

Try telling that to the police. After the world snapped into place I reported the ... particulars.

And?

And I was called everything from a prankster to a killer to delusional. Questioned, grilled, released, and ignored.

And Donnie?

They said he cleared the spit of land beneath the lighthouse and landed in the bay...washed out to sea and ... sucked under the waves.

And you have your doubts?

I think he believed himself somewhere else; he wished himself away.

I have a confession to make.

Hmmm? What?

I've heard this story before. A little differently, of course. But very much the same.

Wha ... really? I just met you, how ...

Do you think we're here, at the "scene of the crime" by accident? Really?

Who told you ...

Donnie did. He flew to my window. After he left here. To ... convert me.

He stole virgin blood from you?

No. Actually, I "stole" it from him. We were ... close, after the fact.

My G... You were lovers?

He was half right. Virgin blood can do wondrous things because desire is greatest before fulfillment, most potent, and delicious ...

Who ...

Would you like closure? Fulfillment?

Your eyes ...

You possess the same desire ... I smell it.

The ground looks closer ...

Would you like to fly?

Pretty Poison

You're kind of
sweet and good,
though that's not
my style.

I need
transcendent anger
to explode
into fistfights
and fornication–
towering sparks
of blissfully intricate desire–
sweet honeyed
blood in every kiss–
that's what I miss–

I need to ride
tumescent rage
through walls,
around the room
in cheap hotels,
parking lots,
cars, buses–
midnights in
the hushed oases
of cemetery tombs,
black and blue–
tenderness to

rage, laugh and claw
the white-hot passion
from the skin. My sin–

I'm never
cruel enough
to finish with my
men–I merely
castrate them
on the sweet
tip of a pen.

If love is a
sickness, then
I'm in love
with the
sickness
I'm in.

On the Downside

I.
    At the base
    of our beings
    there is an ennui
    nothing can erase
    no eloquence can dissever
    no delicacy trace.
    Despite the lovers
    we've embraced
    the coldness in our bones
    never seems displaced
    with dozens of pursuits
    etched into another face.
    In the deadly mirror,
    the stabbing
    piercing sadness
    something commonplace.

II.
    There are those times
    we politely listen
    to the myriad
    troubles of others,
    until we become
    inundated
    with their stale sorrows,
    dragging us deep
    into a smooth
    sleek pit

somewhere between
sleep and death–
We make promises
in good faith
we never
intend to keep.

III.

I'm tired of maintaining myself
or maintaining the illusion
of maintaining myself–
s'okay, though,
be just fine,
always am.

The Way Goes On

I hoped the road
would rise
dove-like
to caress my feet
soothing the sullen
alchemy
of these
twisted streets.

Suffering an oasis
to drift
with a kiss
like dew
onto the path
we'd pledged
as I follow you.

The Apostle's Erection

The wonders of
an agony throbbing
at the bases
of their souls,
a repentance
unknown to them,
foreign to such
self-control–

As feet rush
after them,
their desires bundled
into twine,
rise with ascendant
hunger,
almost divine–

All the pleasures
they abhorred
that seemed to make
the angels sob,
cause grown men
to smile
at the feet
of other gods.

Stepford Lives

You know...

There was this girl: quiet, studious, very bright, and almost soft underneath her armor.

A little church
a little street
a little skeptical
a little tired of doing everything the hard way.

Sat in my class and wrote me a story about doing right by a daughter born to a long gone daddy like a vision of pride.

She wore low cut tops, bracelets, a cross, two fine gold rings and an offering; a shy smile of invitation to her miracle as guest of honor and savior in one, brief fling. Father to an orphaned mother's daughter. An orgasm, tenderness and a shitload of bling.

I love my wife, I'm certain that I do, but sometimes I wish I could be her savior rather than the last rung on a rusted ladder before the darkness sings.

Anyway, this is my resignation, effective immediately. I think someone is waiting for me ...

Underground

Your sandy, salty hands
beneath my shirt
melt away tomorrow–
melt away the hurt–
make the waste places
wet with life,
slithering with softness
just beneath
our eyes.

Let the sun
the sea
the waves
carry me
gently, gently
away.

Sign Language

Fingertips race to taste
the pleasure of your flesh
the sweet geography
my eyes and I caress–
hold me close
until the curvature
of our dark distress
melts into me softly;
my words are
meaningless.

The Mad Story of a True Man

He said if he
put a bullet through
my skull, angels
would dance
on my grave.

He lives to drape
that animal mystique
next to his skin.

He laughs—
he's seen too much
violence, TV—
thinks dreams are
manga, foreign film,
cartoons, pornography.

He claims a slave
mastery, but lately
his fat body seethes
with the low rumble of
rotten lungs.

His
dreams twist like
string round the fingertips
of children crawling
through trash heaps
for treasures they
can't possibly contain–
artifacts they'd sooner
lose than keep.

He's like that–
He likes to hover round,
a gullible son of
unfortunate daughters,
to impress them
before they mock him
in his sleep.

Marionette

If I slit the skull,
pound in the eyes,
gouge the mouth,
form ears from scraps,
lace filaments for hair,
teach the lips to smile,
give the clay mind wit,
teach the articulate ape
to cohabit among tribes
just alike,
would it profane
its place, and
in pure streams
defecate?
Boil in seething ennui
delivering dreams
to hate?
So? I would have
laughed at it
if I hadn't pitied it more:
cast it down before it comes to life, and
to the hell it was intended for.

Witness

She fell from the sixty-third floor of the Sears Tower on a Tuesday morning and lay like a misplaced doll on the roof of a limousine in the courtyard below. I'd like to believe her sleepy-eyed smile in the midst of a blonde tumbleweed meant she'd made peace with whatever fates had led her to shatter a column of air during that sprawling flight to oblivion. A dark dress draped over folds of bent metal that had the shine of velvet made her seem as solemn as a dignitary or a prophetess. Despite a missing shoe, her landing appeared as sudden and as soft as a splash of water. Painless. "Mist and nothingness awaits," an onlooker said. I'd prefer to think she's found a better somethingness beyond this anonymous crowd. Somewhere, some loss has been eased and she's found whatever comfort God's become. Yeah ... well.

I'd like to think she has.

At the Gate

What do you think of
when you're sitting alone
and the air is still
cool as a question
waiting to be formed?
Is it in this moment
time stops,
movement ceases, and
faith in detached
sensation increases?
Is this what is felt
in the altered state
or beyond all power
to elucidate?

Gulliver

As he was staked
to the ground
like a human tent,
a motherly voice
admonished him:
"We don't make rules
to restrict you.
We make rules
to keep you safe.
And by the way,
please don't pee
on my castle."

Eye of the Zombie

He kissed her full lips
with unfelt passion,
called down the stars
that never quite cared,
walked in the world
a sleep deprived minstrel, and
lay down in her arms and
made love in despair.
He found a fine job
with a sizable income,
dreamed that each pretense
was all for the best, and
slowly unwound
with a violent tremor,
a fresh 9/11
in the land of the deaf.

Rearview

You maintained the tone the voice embraces,
spun the errant words round bone and blood,
those that came undone, unmasked mere faces,
and shamed themselves to death and then were done–
rising from the ashes, then gently lifted
even from the earth's frivolous gifts,
treasures through lean fingers, slowly sifted,
as if it were the end. In fact, it is.

Into the Air

A leaf falls–
A ray of light
On a cool October
Morning knifes
Into the air–
Lays a pattern
On the floor.
A leaf falls–
Silently, a faint
Shadow of a
Passing season–
The days grow
Colorful as
Spring flowers,
Briefly
For no reason.
Time, the
Mechanical
Invention of
The over-wise,
Marks nothing,
Means even less
To the ages,
Mirrored in
Men's eyes.

Cinnamon

Lovely young girl's laughter
wreaths the sweet hereafter
with a bit of bliss
better than a kiss.

How could this domain
ever shoulder pain
when every lover's ache
leaves pleasure in its wake?

Fallen

If I were to burn in hell
Would all my whispers
burn as well?
And if I, instead, entered heaven,
Would those whispers be forgiven?

Twilight

Rub my face
Against the night, set
Every star
Hung by string
Soft as silk,
And beaded pearls–

Teach my madness
How to sing
Loveliness
Is where I've been.
Loveliness
Is where you are.
Darkness has
Her paramour, and
I, my bright
And shining star.

Bird of Perfect White Silence

I envisioned a white plain
And a cable of red and blue
Twined down the middle
A subtle horizon
In no real landscape.

I thought I saw a gallery
And imagined people
Wandering
What can it mean?
What had he said?

The colors seemed
So striking such
An odd command
Of blue and red
Such elegance
They said.

I saw myself
In the shadow there
Wondering at the crowd,
And as each of them
Compared the image
To itself

My thoughts
Were drawn to you
And then to no one else.

I dreamed what others
Seldom speak.
I saw,
Although I never sought.

American Dream Therapy

I hope your husband has treated you well,
Your 2.5 children are wholesome and good,
Your middle-class mansion is neat as a pin,
And none of your values are misunderstood.
Otherwise, hush, or the stumbling dark
Will whisper its wit as you slide to your knees,
Wondering when the nightmares had begun,
Slithering with skin like a shocking disease.

Letter to Another Country

The serpentine coils of the narrow road vaulted by torturous degrees to the plateau that held the small village midair in the mist, near the base of the mountain range. He'd often spoken of the terrain as "the Island of West Virginia," yet nothing in the States could claim such exotic beauty; no mountain could be lovely as this, no soil so rich as this volcanic loam, no woman taste as sweet.

It was cooler here. Often in the city the heat rose, dove-like, from every atom of air and each crack in the abused pavement, its stifling grip clutching the throat of the unwary traveler. Those acclimated to the elements would glance curiously at the pale American about to board the train for the long trek to a far different world.

The coffee swirled in each clear glass, a strong Sumatran blend grown on land very close to that of the old couple that shared their home in the small community nestled near the lesser mountains of Kendal Province.

"You haven't changed much," the young man said as he was offered the hot liquid and a bowl of cane sugar to sweeten it.

"Nor you," his host said, smiling, as thin tendrils of vapor slowly danced above the cup.

Dancing was a form of sacrifice, she'd told him, both pleasure and obligation swaying as one.

"How was your trip?" The older man enquired.

"Long. Tiring. Twenty-five hours in the air with little rest. The usual."

"You'll be wanting a shower then," his host commented. "We'll warm the water on the stove."

"Thank you. I believe I'll feel a bit more human after that."

"Your wife said you weren't feeling well?"

The young man shook his head.

"Your daughter can't keep a secret," he said.

"She's concerned."

"I know, so am I. Nothing seems beautiful anymore. It all melts into sameness." He smiled humorlessly. "Like sugar in coffee."

"But the sugar is sweet and the coffee is warm."

"I can't seem to feel either of those," the young man shrugged. "I don't belong anywhere."

"You belong with your wife," the old man replied.

"I belong to her," the young man corrected. "My vows."

"Mean nothing if your soul no longer honors them."

"No doubt," the young man sighed.

"Why did you marry my daughter?" the elder challenged.

"Because…."

"Because?"

"I loved her. Love her, I mean."

"Hm?"

The coffee had long ceased dancing, the cups cooled and empty. The muddy grounds had settled like silt.

"You were nineteen when you married?" The young man asked. "And your wife was fifteen?"

"Yes. We were young," the elder smiled ruefully. "And poor."

"How did you know it was the right decision?"

"We didn't just know. We believed."

"An act of faith?"

"Something like that."

The young man's eyes gradually closed, and a slow century later, he replied with his own rueful smile.

"She wishes you would stay," his host said abruptly.

"I'm sorry?"

"She wishes you would stay," he repeated.

"My wife?"

"My wife," the elder smiled.

The young man was stunned.

"Really? I thought she disliked me."

"She doesn't understand you. Perhaps no more than you understand yourself. But you have become our son. You've married our daughter."

"After five years she thinks of me as family? I'm.."

"Speechless?" The elder grinned.

"Yes. Papa, you've always respected me and I've appreciated that more than you know. But, Mama ... Thank you both."

The elder nodded.

"Your wife is calling. Are you feeling well?"

"Well enough. Terimah kasih."

"So?" His wife said; arms crossed. The hotel was a hive of activity.

"So?"

"The conversation? What was it about?"

"You, me, us, them, everything."

"And?"

He shrugged. The habit of answering questions with questions had become an unavoidable means of delaying the inevitable; like a firing squad composed of octogenarians, death came slowly, understanding even more slowly.

"They know so much and so little," he said quietly.

"What?"

"Your father," he replied. "I've never respected anyone as much as I respect him. When we disagree we do so gently, it's his nature. But your mom ..."

"Has she upset you?"

"No, she shocked me. Before I left to meet you she hugged me and called me 'son.'"

"What!"

"Your mother kissed my cheek and claimed me as a son."

"That's wonderful!" His wife said with a smile reminiscent of her father's broad grin.

"That's a maelstrom of emotion," he mused. "Amazing!" His thoughts coiled, flexed and relaxed as easily as a cat that had found a sill to sun itself. Now, three hours distant from his in-law's small house, his thoughts pursued him.

She sat next to him on the edge of the bed, the two of them silent as the bustling staff of the hotel prepared rooms, washed linens, greeted guests and served Asian cuisine in the dining room. Perpetually busy, always smiling.

He held her hand absently.

"I love you," he said.

"You do?" His wife asked in a mocking tone.

"Of course," he said.

"You're not saying that because you should? Because we're married?"

"No."

"Hm," she considered the declaration carefully, as if weighing its value against that of a precious stone.

"I've always thought you were beautiful," he said.

"If you say that again you'll embarrass me," she smiled.

"What?"

She turned toward him slowly and took his hand.

"If you tell me I'm beautiful you'll embarrass me," she repeated firmly.

"Why should that embarrass you?" He asked.

"Because if I'm lovely, your touch should tell me so. Not your words."

"I see. We're books then, and love and beauty are forms of Braille?"

"Of course. And unread books yield no secrets."

"Oh," he exhaled as the mystery of their marriage crept slowly back into his bones. His thoughts began to chase the memories huddled in the corners of his soul. Like mice, they scurried from the light.

"Is this a new language we're about to learn?" He asked breathlessly.

"Hush," the soft voice warned as the mirror of the inner kingdom convulsed and he was swallowed whole.

The old man sat, sipping tea, as the workers wrestled the precious cargo from the truck and deposited it in the house. He smiled, pleased with himself, as he surveyed what would soon be the island of another culture nestled in their home. For as long as his daughter and son-in-law cared to claim it, and as often as they cared to visit, this marriage chamber would remain to welcome them in its own way, and theirs.

"Smooth enough," he affirmed, nodding at the rough stones that adorned the walk like slices of glass on gravel.

"Clean enough," he thought as the red clay at the gate, packed tight as asphalt, was swept of twigs and leaves and the tiled floor gleamed seraphic white.

"Good enough," he concluded, as the new bed and its magnificent headboard teetered on the ancient truck in the narrow drive, waiting to be placed in the hallowed room.

"May you be blessed with believing above knowing," the elder silently prayed, wiping tears from his eyes. "Blessed be."

Good enough.

When Beauty Met the Beast

The saddest song
on earth
is the one we
never hear,
because we're
transfixed
on the barb of
someone else's
melody.

Our own
symphonies
seem spare
as an Amish
dressing gown,
or the simple path
of a child's plaited hair.
Just one more thing
to do, before I drop
the other shoe;
stretch out, relax
in feline
solitude.

Happiness is
such a drag,
when you're
trying to

sing the blues ...

But if that's not
the case, make haste.
Add another fool
to the race
whose leaden
legs have
nothing left
to prove.
C'est la vie
On dit
Let's go,
Tout de suite.

The Conversation

It's been awhile,
long enough to
seem polite ...

Yeah, well I
gotta get in
the car and
go with
these people
someplace ...

But I'll–
no, not now;
maybe when
the planets realign,
the heavens melt
and harden into
dreams laced
with nostalgia
with sour offerings,
the earth bows
at your discretion,
and I become
reacquainted
with the trick that
turned two
bodies into one, and
maybe then I'll come.

Speaking so openly
is the same escapade as
our swift whisper past
half opened doors
full of drama
I never paid
the privilege for,
with dust gathered
on every kiss,
and every chained embrace
an empty metaphor,
a third resurrection
of this hopelessness
would seem
remiss, abhorred.

I can't do
this–
it's not that
it isn't
interesting,
it is–
I just wish
it was
what it
could have
been
Later.
What?
I'll do what's most
appropriate, I guess:
shall I garland
your neck
with a gentle
kiss, or

bite your lip
with a brutal
wish?

Sleep Studies

He was like a man who discovered his past by accident in a haze of heroin he'd boiled and poured into his eyes. We were afraid of him but we wanted to respect him even though he'd collapsed his veins and wore shades to protect his bloodshot orbs. My mother prayed because there wasn't any other hope for us. We were a near fatherless group of four living in a trailer a mile outside of town, but Mom never complained about our bastard lives. He loved us with a deadbeat father's half-hearted devotion, and I'm sure he was always gone to keep us from the line of fire.

They found him in a ditch when I was eleven, and we buried him in another with the help of a local church where Mom spent most of her time. She was the exhausted demigod to Dad's total devil, but we were too young to know why she was tired. Now she rests the way an angel might that had outlasted hell.

If only we could learn to sleep so furiously.

War Games

Tell me, when the plot
was written, scribbled
in blood before hungry
eyes manipulating the
tiny flesh-bound pieces
of the chessboard;
was any of this a grim surprise?
Did beauty rise on the current
of an unfamiliar dawn? Did
you have a good life, when
you died? Enough to base
a movie upon?

Imaginary Lover

She wore her
belly like a bloated
badge, proud
to be the recipient
of such seed as
pleased her dark,
demonic lover;
wailing and imperious,
a tower of need–
imagined in
such vivid
detail, the man
became another migraine,
a sort of ethereal thing.

She let drop the
cool pillow and
became a girl
drifting in an
abyss no
tongue could
sing.

Auto Focus

If we wait
too long, shadows
overtake us; the
contrasts that create
delicate contours vanish–
bodies melt before souls
envelop ecstasy, kissed amiss
by the alchemy of
ordinary life–
nothing remains–
and purity is neither
gray nor black nor white,
bit mapped in the
obscure calligraphy
of unexamined wonders
pooled in the sweet
palmistry of night.

Outward Bound

If I should someday
clot with dust,
a cast iron pump
smothered with rust,
my blood coalesce
into thick tributaries,
fraudulent experience retreat
as those who pledge
yet seldom marry;
would there be a sound
a scream, mourning? or
would mourning seem,
as copious tears,
unnecessary? I'm told
Hell is where this river's flowing;
as if my sad ship
were derelict, stripped of
her sails and had no
means of rowing.
In my dreams,
I have a way of knowing.
I have a way of knowing.

The Beloved Object

Could she be
perfect as an
aqua-mottled vase,
the dust of forgotten
kingdoms, fallen
walls, bits of
pottery from Thrace?

Is she poetry, an
Aeneid, the verse
of an ancient
tongue, common
as an apostle's
contemporary when
that same empire
was young?

Could she stir
the ashes of an
army, place
thoughts on
a lover's tongue?
Pool all her
pretty tears together
and rise like another sun?

City on the Edge of Forever

Life seems a
tempting blend
of 'must haves'
and 'don't needs'
the twisted whip of
acquaintance, friendship,
enmity, compulsive desires,
jealousy, death,
base elements, greed.

Strolling the strand
of some denuded beach,
baked bones litter a bleached
shoreline, corpse strewn sands,
blood stained coral reefs;
it must have been an Eden once,
it must have surpassed
the seer's dream, before Hell
foreclosed on Heaven,
stole her loveliness,
stripped the temple
of her priest.

Foundations plowed,
ravaged gates, a multitude of
wonders lost, innocence deceased,
another Eden's necessities,
wannabes that must

desperately be ignored
even as their kisses disagree.

Tragic Kingdom

I.

I think she told me her dad died holding her hand and wearing a diaper as he slowly surrendered to cancer like a child to punishment. Maybe it was just the delirium of experiencing strength reduced to soft clay as she massaged back muscles that no longer existed, or maybe it was the fact that they shouted whatever prayers they knew like threats at the ceiling as his chest arched twice to heaven before sinking into the shell he'd once been, but she still exhibits some profoundly tragic skills. A finer Ophelia, a more inane Anna Nicole, I've never met. She'd like to believe we're all bastards for believing something better will emerge from the cesspool of this nanosecond, but the numbness of now will become the numbness of then as time melts into time. Eventually, depression will evict her from his house like a slum lord and she'll either recover or find a new reason to haunt bars and emulate Knievel and Icarus.

II.

The world is full of tragic actresses who never needed to audition for the chaos that they lived, but there are a few who found peace under the rainbow. Sometimes any sort of action is a good thing, even an impossible war against deity grinds the armor to paper thin plates; the kind we record our confessions on. The last time either of us saw God, He was drunk, lost, and frightened. The exact image we expected to find over the sink and in the soul. We met, married, drank, regretted, and sobered up. I think we'll both be better now. As better as we can be. Anyway, she's pregnant and I pray that, somehow, our daughter will enjoy her innocence like a bright toy and become the covenant we lost.

Island of Lost Luggage

I come from a land of
unclaimed packages,
where sentiment is
silly and cold and
old men in colorless robes
expound unhinged philosophies
littering the slim
skin of distant seas:
but you're soft as a tartan quilt.

I come from a land of
impenetrable anomalies,
where crook-fingered
spider veined intelligentsia
dwell, neutered in the
cool manner of adding
machines cast in a
Boolean hell
where love is neither
quantified nor felt:
yet I marvel at your smile.

I come from a land of
unsung soliloquies,
where children chained
to exemplary degrees
by divine persuasion pluck
sunlight from their sockets

bow non-calloused knees before
human devils' withering agendas
engendering a similar abuse:
despite the scars.

I would have chosen you.
I might have clustered among
crushed roses with them,
if their frail beauty
hadn't whispered what to do.

Sympathy for the Devil

Multitudes funneled
through the checkpoint
of oblivion, dragging
dolls in childlike hands,
briefcases of businessmen;
rattling knife-like
piles of pavement
stone, vacant eyes
scorched, flesh moans
a paean, some
promise of dignity
forever lost, visionary
windows socketless,
brevity dripped from
dirty cheeks, dementia,
tongues torn, lips
too numb to speak;
an empire's smitten eulogy.

The promontory of
divine inertia grown helpless,
unknown;
unknowable
collage
of stories
scraped from tombs–
life imitating life.

We seem to speak
in tongues of dust.
Has the ark
of some
covenant
come to us?

I Am the Night. That Is My Name.

Slender as a cinnamon stick
with rich hues of mahogany,
"I am velvety dusk," she said.
"I am the dawn's epiphany."

"Think of me as a wordless tune,
my children a bright refrain,
and every Endymion strand of hair
an elegy stars contain."

"How do our wiles define description?
Before language ever shivered the tongue,
thought strode ashore at my discretion,
kissed logic and came undone."

Baghdad Cafe

So is this
the torture you
intended? This
blowtorch to
the balls, this
rapt intrusion?

The squeal
of slaughtered hogs
caught in a house fire
boiled to the bone's
tormented fusion.

A weeping child's
anti-catechism,
the skull below
the hammer's
majesty,
borne upon
the backs of
crueler kingdoms,
hymnals of a
lesser pedigree.

Is this the grand mal
seizure of
the senses?

Recompensed in
nightmares, impaled
in dreams.
I thought I knew
the souls of
sad enchanters
slick non sequiturs
in narrow streets.

I saw a hollow
child, nude and
filthy, staring down
the magi's withering
greed, with a beggar's
dance and death descending
clattering a cup
in simmering need.

An end that
seemed unblessed
as its beginning,
visionary madness
stood aloof,
whispering 'There's
crimson death
in heaven.' As they
felt a world's
divine reproof.

epitaph

myron terle
cubicle drone
fiftysomething
midwest ...
let us search, then,
the magic pattern
of the soul's sudoku
as fingertips trace
an unblemished
shoreline
in ancient prophecies
of regret–
he was a failure
his entire life
having never accomplished
an eternal goal, nor sated
any sacred dream–
he believed obituary babbling
to be inane bullshit
sold to the quivering masses
of grief-stricken unfortunates
in the midst of loss and shock,
propping false memories
to a fallen god (although his family
thought it best to tell tender lies
of wondrous accomplishment
with vigor and a nervous smile)–
for the purpose of making

earthly goods ascend
to heaven on sinister wings
for the simple ditch,
he preferred in place of a well
kept grave–he asked these few
lines be scrawled in slate
on the broken pavement
he called home–
"he was born
he lived awhile
he died
amen–"
drink up

Absurdistan

They taught us to curse
angels at the college,
to hurl varied imprecations
at the dead;
simple as a stone
might shatter glass,
we knew no sylvan being
could exist. Hadn't all
the magi told us so?
How could pristine intellect
be wrong?
We'd prayed to fame
and convened a seance for holy wit,
catalogues of the quoted
led us here, no mystic
could be closer
to the truth, or else
both quote and quoted
are the same.
Let me sip the nectar
of pronouncement over fact
I think I'll sleep a little better
knowing less, curled here
in a comforter of bliss
as sweet ennui melts
into the cracks.
...I could have told you
no cartel ever named

could quantify the hunger
that we claim ...

when parallel lines intersect

    This poem cannot fully express its intricacies because art skims like mist on waters that cannot grasp meaning quickly enough to register depth to any profound degree.
    This poem would prefer to be a leisurely wave caressing a tidal shore as it rests against the sands of distant lands and laps up images of stars.
    This poem would love to sit quietly in the back row of a foreign cinema absorbing the swirling fractals of a film as geometric as a nightscape by Van Gogh.
    This poem wants to be a stiletto drive by's whispered threat as a stunned eyewitness spills a slurpee on his shoe.
    This poem wishes it had said/done/been more.
    This poem wishes it had asked more probing questions.
    This poem wishes it could be a semi-psychotic preamble to greater strangeness.
    This poem, like a stirring madness, will never be complete.
    This poet will never be finished ...

So Far Away from Here

Africanus delectus;
te quiero, mi amor. What
other form of discourse
need there be? I sought
audience with self-deluded
poets whose lips shared
neither self nor poetry.
Then I saw a sliver
of dark magic, the whisper
of a slender camisole;
as moonlight bathed
the armor of Medea
in the pantheon
of wonders that she stole.
Pooled in paths of ancient
labyrinthine kingdoms, feathered
notes caressed imperial wind
till colored rain fell
from a candied heaven,
and fastened to the souls
they'd hoped to bless.
If love is not
the kiss of simple
reason, then where
is the reason
that we seek.

Dialogue

    1. Lost Gospel Blues
if this incurable sadness
hadn't nipped at my heels,
my bloated soul might lie
in silk, rather than
in an alley shrieking
as the DT's made real
imagined and
imagined fact
... I'd like another sip
of that fine brew–
the glorious bitterness
takes me back
to the fled nest
and forsaken forest;
I'll cling to that mystery
like a sustaining rail

    2. Cyclysm
I believe hidden beneath
the track lighting
of your soul
there exists some
nebulous philosophy;
an animal fear in
an Armani shell,
committed to the wind
like a leafy stream

based on the odds
of this slim prediction.
I'll take a nap
near that paradigm;
like a fearless farmhand
among half-framed labors
have some camembert, mon ami
and a fine white whine.

Statesman

I'm a statesman
I'm a state statesman
I'm a statesman.
I'm a real gone guy
with some voodoo style
I'm a statesman.
I tease infoholics
like a toreador,
ship dreams to oblivion
on distant shores,
stir violent mobs
like sweet bitches
and whores;
I am a statesman.
Someone should really love me
before the point is moot
they should be prancing
to my mantra
in a tailored suit
I'm a statesman
I'm a state statesman
I'm a statesman.
Well I'm Likud cool
I'm a shining jewel
I'm a statesman.
Each nuclear assumption
is a blistering wail,
disappointment and doubt

are swiftly beaten and jailed–
your Eden may be lovely
mine is razor and nails;
I am a statesman.

Creditorial

Why do you do this to me? Why
do you continue to construct
these befuddling puzzles as
if cyphers were scripture
and a shaman's dilemma
were a source of hope?
To what encrypted logic
do you cling?
And your point is?
Sharp as a dagger thrust
through the heart!
Why haven't you
discovered style is substance?
Don't you like manga? Martial arts
wifi? The world wasn't made
for the intellectual sort!
I write what's there.
And where has that left us?
As if hacks and fanboys weren't
enigma enough. You need to be
Agassi before winning mattered.
I write with the patience
of God on hiatus. By the way,
I can't recall arguing with
a mirror before.

Buried Pleasure

all beauty is
emptiness, although
each word is lovely, and
your page remains naked,
a seraphic white stain.
each mighty attempt
at prose lapsed
to poetry, each
boisterous intonation
became a framed
first print.
what could be
lovelier than
this grand illusion, lush
as a ripe fig
about to be won?

Triptych

The Bow is Drawn–
I expected a mother's love
and received a father's wrath.
I've long since disowned
both those twisted
souls, but
this agony is Herculean,
pulling the temple down
as certain as some Samson
died to purify himself,
even as Delilah danced
cruel and nude.
He lay down the pen, frowned,
wished he were truly tired …
that wouldn't do at all–
I write what's in front of me;
darkness, death, the old nemesis
fallen in a palsied crawl,
amnesiacs bathed in crisp
white dread as cherubim
upward fall.
It won't do
Now…
What will?
The Arrow Flies–
Sorry, I
haven't been a better
friend, we disagree

on almost everything
and our arguments
are often cataclysmic,
but I'd sacrifice my life
to soothe you, I'd
take a bullet for your opinion
despite how frequently
our stars may have misaligned;
years ago I might have said
'I love you,' now
the best I can give
is time.
The Arrow Falls–
So what have you composed?
A suicide note.
That's nice. What's it about?
Three pages too long.
I've a huge list of friends.
Any last wishes? I mean now
that you're leaving?
That you might leave with me
and cushion the blow.

The Stone Garden

... the young man leapt
toward Valhalla above
as if a swimmer
were treading wind
clawing a column
of shattered air
as he met the embrace
of the furious earth
descending the ladder
toward oblivion's kiss
foregoing the safety
of his perch ...

Fable

Once upon a time there lived a poet named Renaldo. He enjoyed composing stories and poems to entertain friends, although very few people could grasp the oddities he wrote.

"Renaldo," they would say, "you have a wondrous grasp of language, for your words flow like sweet waters from an everlasting stream."

"But, Renaldo," they continued with shrugs of resignation, "as lovely as this seems to the senses we cannot understand it. Pray tell us, what do these silly phrases mean?"

"What do they mean?" Renaldo replied, befuddled. "The meaning's as plain as peasant food."

"For you perhaps. For us it's a mystery that causes our eyes to cross. You write riddles, Renaldo."

"Write something simpler and we'll listen," they added as they left.

Renaldo thought a very long time about what the villagers had said. Perhaps they were right. Perhaps poems should be plain and songs should sing themselves. Perhaps ...

So Renaldo shed the guise of the poet he once was, and despite sleepless nights and a hill of crumpled paper, he codified his thoughts and became wealthy as a king.

Then all his friends were thrilled, for the magic of his words now required little labor to be fully understood.

And the walls of his domain glittered like the hidden jewels his mind had once conceived when his visions had been dreams.

Life was fat and easy.

But Renaldo wasn't happy and nothing could appease him. His new status left him empty and his challenges were few. What was wonderful was hollow as his castle's unused rooms or his many statuettes.

So he sought the sage advice of a mentor in the mountains who babbled quite a lot and occasionally made sense.

The old man listened quietly as Renaldo detailed his dilemma, pausing to mumble words as odd as those Renaldo used to write.

"My God, write what's in front of you!" The old man finally shouted. "I say screw the critics! Else logic's just a lovely bird that sings a fetid song."

"'Do your best to be yourself. That's what I would have answered, if you had had the sense to ask the second question first."

Renaldo thanked the hermit for this bitter admonition that a dozen others echoed on at least as many mountains.

"Perhaps it's time," he said, "to truly be immortal. After all the man is measured by his very last pen stroke."

So he sadly scaled the stairs of the vast estate he'd founded; he, unable to choose between his comforts and his literary soul.

He leapt into the darkness toward an unforeseen conclusion, and caromed like a bullet off a group of men below.

"How fortunate to have landed on such a worthy group of tourists," he said of the friends who'd tried to change him long ago.

Slipping his credentials into the pocket of the nearest, he allowed the world to mourn his passing as he disappeared into the darkness and became another man.

Buoyed by the broken bodies that had broken his fall, Renaldo melted into the mists of obscurity to become a legendary poet and a somewhat better writer.

And the dead lived happily ever after.

~Finis~

Bill Suter was born on November 30, 1959 in Warren, Ohio. Married to his muse and angel, who prefers to remain anonymous. Graduate of Youngstown State University (YSU) in Youngstown, Ohio with a master's degree in technical writing. He has been a writer for at least 50 of his 60 years on earth, and a teacher of writing for the last decade and a half, at both YSU and Eastern Gateway Community College. Before becoming a full-time writer/instructor, he was a laborer for 20 years at several local aluminum plants that have long since closed their doors. He says if he were sane, he would spend more time at rest and less time at his desk, but the itch to write is always present. And so, it goes.

www.ingramcontent.com/pod-product-compliance
Lightning Source LLC
Chambersburg PA
CBHW071317080526
44587CB00018B/3257